Along the Way

Along the Way

COLLECTED POEMS & PROSE

Scott Pariseau

▲
Rain Mountain Press
New York City

Copyright 2022 by Scott L. Perrizo (aka Scott Pariseau)

All rights reserved. No part of this book may be used or reproduced in any form whatsoever without written permission of the author, except in the case of reviews or other critical articles, especially if they bring healing.

ISBN: 978-1-7337916-4-9

Rain Mountain Press
www.rainmountainpress.com

Cover and text design: Scott Pariseau
Cover photograph: Mira Perrizo
Printing: Gray Dog Press

Printed in the United States of America

To the memory of my parents,
Marvin & Beverly,
who loved & nurtured me,
instilled in me a love
of books & the natural world;

to the memory of my cousin,
Mitchel Perrizo, Jr.,
for his interest & support,
for helping me better know
my own history;

to Dr. Joseph Amato,
author, mentor,
fellow poet & more —
for a lifetime of
friendship & support.

Contents

Acknowledgments viii
Author's Preface x
Prelude xi
Night Walk, Winter 1
Night in Harkey Valley, Arkansas 3
Summer's Eve 4
Waiting for Snow 5
After Great-Grandfather's Funeral 6
Last Visit 7
In Rotation 9
Still Life 10
fragment 11
A Dog's Morning Prayer 12
First Crush 13
In Autumn Light 14
Night Sky in Winter 15
At Ocean Haven 16
Dream at Ocean Haven 18
In the Wink of an Eye 19
When Crocuses Break Ground 20
Haiku at Dusk 21
Humility in Fall 22
Thirteen Turtles: A Prose Meditation 23
In the Garden 26
House Off Peebly Road 27
First Snow 31
Her Hair 34
My Great Cat Clovis, Afternoon Snow 36

April Dawn 37
Night light 38
The life of dreams 39
Cold Spring 40
Marble 41
Year's End 43
Spring Snowstorm 44
Marble Morning 45
Patio in Albi 46
At Crestone Park 48
werewolves in deep night 49
Prairie Sunset 51
Poem on a morning with jam 52
The Wedding 53
1. Two White Feathers Fell From Sky 54
2. Two White Feathers Fell From Sky 57
What's In a Name? 58
Autumn Dawn 76
Our Evolution 77
A New Year 80
A Poet's Epitaph 82
About the Author 85

Acknowledgments

The publication of this work would not be possible without the many contributions of the publishers, Stephanie Dickinson and Rob Cook at Rain Mountain Press, and first acknowledgments go to them. Their intelligent and helpful suggestions, encouragement, extreme patience, and obvious passion for their work have made this publishing process a unique honor in my life. I am very grateful to join the list of quality books and authors at Rain Mountain Press.

To Stephanie Dickinson in particular I owe many thanks for her careful reading, helpful critiques, and encouraging comments of various drafts I've sent her over the years, many included in this book. Without such important support, this work would have never found its way to publication.

I am thankful for the contributions to my writing of my late friend and pigeon buddy, poet and teacher Dr. Donovan Welch of Kearney, Nebraska. Don and I exchanged many phone calls and emails about our beloved pigeons and many early and late drafts of poems. Don's great knowledge and love for poetry and prosody and his insights were freely shared and gratefully received, and I greatly miss our friendly exchanges and occasional visits.

I want to thank my sister Gail Perrizo for her reading of some of the pieces and especially her suggestions on the "What's In a Name" piece and for telling me the story of the Minneota Icelanders.

Many thanks to Mira Perrizo for advice and help in various ways, especially her careful reading of the prose pieces and suggested corrections, her help with preparing the final files, plus her photo used for the cover.

I want to acknowledge the important part the informal group for the Perrizo family history project, initiated by the late Mitchel Perrizo Jr., played in helping me build my story of family and name — especially Bill Hoffman, Dr. Gordon Berry and Dr. Mary Hynes-Berry. Our travels together and shared interest resulted in research and information that changed the story for all of us.

Good friend and masterful writer Rosalind Palermo Stevenson graciously read various poems and offered excellent comments for their improvement, for which I am very grateful.

To fellow writer Caroline Parizeau in Montréal — my cousin, confidante, and frequent muse — I owe many thanks and much appreciation for her remarkable insights as a reader at the deepest levels and for her valuable suggestions that improved various pieces included here.

As with any act in one's life, conscious or unconscious, there are many forces and people involved in the process; I apologize for not mentioning anyone who contributed in some way to the process of preparing this book. And any other errors or omissions in this collection are indeed the fault and responsibility of the author.

Scott Pariseau
January 2022

Author's Preface

This collection of selected writing is presented nearly chronologically, as the poems and prose pieces represent writings from nearly my lifetime and are presented roughly in the order they were written over many years. Thus, the collection perhaps earns its title, *Along the Way*.

An exception is made for one poem — I am not including it with the other poems that follow and will offer an explanation as to why. The poem, "Fall Migration," was actually the first poem I wrote, it was submitted in its original form as assignment for high school Senior English class. As that, it was written in what was hoped to be an acceptable meter and form for that class and the writing was necessarily both stylized and not entirely my natural voice. The poem later benefited from revisions, though still mainly adhered rather closely to the original. And at one point, my mom had asked me to use the poem as a memorial to my dad, although the original poem was written before his death. For that reason alone, it has value for me and merits inclusion in this book. As its language and style still set it a bit apart from the later poems, I am including it before the others, as a *Prelude*, and hope that this order will make some sense to more than just me.

Scott Pariseau
January 2022

Prelude

Fall Migration
In Memory of Marvin J. Perrizo
(14 February 1928 – 25 November 1971)

Anticipating, I've often stood
in mottled brush near brumous wood
on frosted mornings in the Fall,
listening to the wild geese call.

These feathered spirits in full flight,
just risen now from restive night —
on ancient, airy paths they wing,
foreordained by blood in vein.

In rushes clothed I humbly gaze . . .
Above, dark shapes slip through the haze;
Pure freedom I may witness then,
while watching from that watery fen —

To hear their haunting, lonely cry
come drifting down through cloudy sky,
I long that I might leave the ground
to fly with geese by time unbound.

Along the Way

Night Walk, Winter

I was less than four then,
fit the shovel's scoop,
rode as on a sleigh, while
my Dad ran ahead,
pulling by its handle.

Sprays of snow stuck
to my moist, scarved mouth,
scratched past my face;
above, stars were notched deep
into night's dark sky.
Rabbits raced ahead in moonlit ditches,
criss-crossed the road —
a bustling of shadows,
powdery bursts of snow.

Telephone lines
pulsed overhead —
loud, distinct buzzes
of various pitches
my Father said
could be my Mother and
Grandmother, talking.

We sensed that,
heard maybe voices,
Grandma laughing,
even our names spoken —

then tumbled by wind,
sifted downward
through snow.

Night in Harkey Valley, Arkansas

This family, spread by miles,
is together again, talking late
at the table.   Love stirs,
grows in the eyes
of three generations.

Ancestors are named —
they are present, waiting;
their bones slide easily
into fresh young cousins.

Summer's Eve

I think
I'll fire up
the charcoal briquettes,
   he said;

sit out back,
   maybe water
      the lawn.

Waiting for Snow

Ragged gray clouds
have swept the sky
all day.
Late afternoon,
in cold November light,
I sit by the window
drinking coffee, warming
my hands on the cup.
Winds shriek and moan,
rattle throughout the house.

Corn is gone,
fields are plowed,
trees stripped of leaves —
nothing hinders
the northwest wind!
Gazing west,
toward the great-skyed Dakotas,
I feel the loneliness
that is Winter
on these plains.

After Great-Grandfather's Funeral
(Walking With My Father)

    Dusk so thick
       in Summer,
as we walked out
    through it,
    with crickets
ringing sundown.
Inside, his wife
      still cried;
later, slashed their
    favorite painting.

The breeze came up,
    shook the lilac;
   I shivered when
     you cupped
    your hands,
      blew low,
those notes, then
   I laughed how
   it worked with
the Mourning Dove
   cooing back.

Last Visit
(for Tilda Tone)

There was a hole
  in the wall
    upstairs in one
      bedroom, and in
        the open closet
      where nothing hung
    a piece of ceiling
      had fallen, where
        one could hear
          wind from the attic,
        wires scraping
        the roof above.

On a bedroom floor,
  a framed painting
    lay face-down —
  a tear showed on
    the wallpaper above,
      in a square that remained
      pink in a room turned
    a dirty lavender.

There was nothing
  but debris —
newspapers, endless
  clumps of hair,

    the smell of dust
      nearly alive.

At the kitchen sink,
  the raised
  pump handle
    hung motionless,
      cobwebs dangling.

Light failing,
  we left.
The house
 could be sold,
   or left empty;
there was nothing
  more to be done.

I thought of Tilda,
ancient and gently mad,
 at the back hedge,
  waiting for
  her cat who
    would never
    return home —
"It's dusk I expect him"
     — waiting.

In Rotation

Six puppies,
slurping water
from a bowl —
like a spoked wheel
rotating slowly
clockwise
as they drink.

Still Life

In the searing heat of middle afternoon,
the dry air has become thin and brittle
in the closed, dusty room where
the blinds are drawn; and there
in the dim yellow light,
the moist scent
of cut roses in a bowl
permeates everything.

fragment

To utter your name
  is to begin
   a prayer, or
    to mouth
   an incantation.

A Dog's Morning Prayer

Do with this day
whatever you please —
just give me good scents
on the breezy breeze.

First Crush
(for B)

Laughter embellished emboldened lips, reds streaked
the bounce of auburn hair wrapped 'round
her cinnamon-dusted, burnished cheek,
while her girlish body danced across ground
with pulse and vibrant charge so wild,
I felt all knocked around. When she snapped her fingers
in greeting and unisoned my name, my child's
shyness burned unbearable shame, lacking any answer.

So, that night I pondered how already I'd lost
this older girl to fate, and at what cost,
when circumstance and time conspire,
allowing love to tweak, then goad one higher,
until by consequence they rescind
love, easy as snow is shaped by wind.

In Autumn Light

Behind darkened
foothills, the
back ranges
are lit in
crisp relief.
Rain paints
grass greener
than Spring.
Crows
fly slow,
like black soil
rolling
off plows.
Clarity lingers,
preceding
first frost.

Night Sky in Winter

February, the new millennium.
Every evening I walk
the snowy road as
Sirius scuttles cold claws
across the western sky.

I've become aware that
my remaining life
spins round me
with gathering force.

These familiar constellations,
near and far, nightly
roll slowly across the sky,
impervious — our matter, our
dust, an utter insignificance;
yet perhaps, through
distance, across time, an
impalpable synchronicity.

At Ocean Haven
10 July 2003

At dusk, I perch
in the wide, screened
window of my room.
Far below,
surf crashes in
as mist seeps up
the rugged cove
just north.

A mile offshore,
orange lights on crab boats
bob into focus,
then disappear —
reappear, hazy,
then dip again
to emerge bright,
clear.

In near darkness,
the sudden, swift flight
of a bat
or small bird
startles, breaks my revery.

Rising from below,
the sweet scents
of sautéed green pepper,

then garlic, dance
on the evening breezes.

It has been a long and
pleasurable day — yet,
one still bearing
surprises.

Dream at Ocean Haven
3 July 2004

I dream for a moment,
and in the dream,
I am young again —
the light is the pure yellow
of little flowers,
the deep, clear, vibrant blue
of hydrangea globes.

It is enough for me
to feel again
for only a moment
the unsullied expectancy
of those truly young —
upon waking, I quickly
shake myself back to
my appropriate age.

O, when do those
pure colors of youth
begin acquiring
the solemn tints
of the grave?

In the Wink of an Eye

Age, inexorable leveler,
has its way with all.
Even young flirts
and Romeos become
codgers, crones, ancient
white-haired, shuffling men;
their strangely cocked eye,
wink, or goofy grin —
indecipherable as
all that remains
from a youthful mien.

Moulin Lesperty
Parisot, Tarn-et-Garonne, France
August 2005

When Crocuses Break Ground

    The soft flash
    of winter-white
    legs beneath
    the drape of white
    mid-calf skirt
      in retreat
    on this twilight,
    early Spring street
    is like moonlight
    on lapping water,
    scattering off
    the cold backs
    of silvery fishes
      just beneath.

Haiku at Dusk

The insect chorus
in the woods off my back porch —
nearly deafening . . .

Humility in Fall

On the weekend
  the stray dog I call
    Carla came to stay,
      the Summer heat
        was replaced
      by cooler Autumn air,
        with clear light
          and fresh breezes
        that gently shook
        treetops while
        first leaves
          fell to ground.

The ridiculousness of
  parts of my life
    appalls me.
  In this evening's breeze,
  enjoying setting sunlight
  penetrating these woods,
    highlighting branches, leaves,
      reaching into darker spaces,
    I sigh for change
      of season, how
        my small life has
          been touched by
        this splendor
        far more often
          than I've deserved.

Thirteen Turtles: A Prose Meditation

On a morning walk last week, my dogs led me to an overgrown ditch running along our deserted country road, lush in late Spring verdancy. Nearly covered by long grass, I discovered there thirteen turtles, very recently dead, stacked and fitted neatly together in the small ditch with enough care to avoid detection; most likely, no one but me would ever find them there. A single bullet had pierced each of their shells — a small, neat hole likely from a small-bore firearm, perhaps .22-caliber, suggesting kids, perhaps recently out of school for Summer, bored, looking for "sport." Yet the careful stacking suggests surreptitiousness, perhaps even guilt for the deed after some blood-lust wore away, by an adult instead. I've seen a single turtle at this spot on the road before — to find thirteen indicates some diligence.

Considered *yin* to the phoenix's *yang* in ancient Chinese cosmological symbolism, the turtle was revered in Chinese culture as being one of the world's four sacred beasts, along with the mythical dragon and phoenix and the very real tiger.

Buffalo, one of the most magnificent symbols of North America's natural splendor, were revered by the Native American Plains Tribes before westward expansion by mainly European immigrants nearly ended existence for both these earlier inhabitants of the sweeping expanse of the Great Plains. The equally incredible grizzly bears and wolves, feared for their prowess as natural predators to private livestock herds allowed to graze freely on public lands, were nearly exterminated in the lower forty-eight states by the early twentieth century due to bounties placed on their pelts that were the result of effective lobbying by ranching interests protecting their bottom line.

Passenger Pigeons perhaps represent our saddest and most complete act of species extermination — so numerous was this native bird that passing flocks were said to darken skies for days and the weight of night-roosting birds brought down tree limbs. An Ontario flock in 1886 was estimated to have been a mile wide and three hundred miles long, containing three-and-a-half billion birds, with the flock taking fourteen hours to pass a single point.[1]

As a flock animal in North America, Passenger Pigeons were second in numbers only to the Rocky Mountain Locust, yet they passed out of existence in an amazingly short period after contact with the new settlers of North American lands. Habitat destruction contributed to their initial decline in the early to mid-nineteenth century, as massive deforestation for farming cleared away their roosting areas. But, due to their numbers and the relative ease with which the tightly roosting birds could be taken, mechanized commercial hunting ensured their near complete destruction in the nineteenth century's later years — the meat was considered so inexpensive that it was often the only food of slaves and servants and was used as hog feed, even soil fertilizer. The

---

[1] Ehrlich, Paul R.; Dobkin, David S.; Wheye, Darryl (1988). *The Passenger Pigeon*. Stanford University Press.

last known Passenger Pigeon, named Martha, died in the Cincinnati Zoo on September 1, 1914.

Of these billions of birds that shared our North American skies not long ago, barely survives even memory of their existence today. I ponder the fate of other species irrevocably diminished or senselessly annihilated, the present fate of birds, butterflies, insects, and others with little chance of surviving in our modern world.

Last week I found thirteen dead turtles neatly stacked in a ditch and continue to wonder "*Why?*"

12 June 2012

Sources: The Passenger Pigeon, Ehrlich, Dobkin, Wheye, Stanford University Press, 1988; *Li Po and Tu Fu*, translated by Arthur Cooper, Penguin Classics, 1973, pp. 118–119, "Letter to his Two Small Children Staying in Eastern Lu at Weng Yang Village under Turtle Mountain," poem by Li Po and discussion following, for the material on turtles and their importance in ancient China.

In the Garden

Cardinal's music
  from treetop
throughout the afternoon
    as a male
  throbbed his song.
On the patio
  at dusk,
fireflies by the dozen
   amaze me
  all over again
    with their
   exquisite display.

  O, to be lost in
  this sinuous world
    of bird song
    & bug neon,
     unaware of
    the duplicity
      of men.

House Off Peebly Road
*Upon Hearing My Former Oklahoma Residence
Was Burned To The Ground*

Squatters, the news reported, their warming fire in the wee hours gone out of control. I remember instead the landlord who had pretended to be my friend, monstrous, grossly hairy, bulging belly, imbecilic grin emergent from grubby yellow beard, mouth hung open, tongue flopping in mock ecstasy, as he pretended to light matches with one hand while fake masturbating with the other, to show his love of fire.

Upon inquiring, I'm told by the county sheriff's department detective that no accelerant was found, arson was ruled out, "shoddy worksmanship" was deemed the cause, attic wiring shorting out "over time" finally causing the catastrophe to a relatively new structure. I think back to my weeks before moving out, afraid that my landlord and his partner, the builders and those guilty of the "shoddy worksmanship," were trying to burn down the house while I still lived in it, in order to collect insurance money on a house that was falling apart. While I still lived there, I could conceivably be blamed for a fire.

Every day, I took my laptop to work; when I was asked why, I replied that I knew from "traps" I had set — pieces of clear tape at the inside bottom of exterior doors — that my landlord was making the long drive from town and entering the house in my absence, as the tape was flapping loose from the locked door being opened when I returned home at night, a detail I knew would be beyond this landlord's awareness. I greatly feared that the house would be burned, as they lacked even basic ethics and were intent on collecting insurance; the lives of my resident pets mattered little to them. At work I was asked "What about your pets?" My reply was that I couldn't bring my pets to work, a situation that was an unimaginable horror for me.

Somewhat unbelievably, this was the second fire at that house, as an earlier fire, perhaps less than two years before I moved in, nearly burned it down. Neighbors claimed that the owners/builders had set a fire in order to collect the insurance when their spec house lingered on the market, unsold.

When I had asked my landlord about that earlier fire, a concern because I was living there, he replied evasively to my questioning: "The renter was living there, uh . . . it started in the kitchen; no, maybe the renter wasn't there then, I think it was empty." This vague recollection, as if from the distant past, was about a fire less than two years previous, in a house not yet four years old, with charred rafters in the attic visible through their disguise of a recent coating of white paint (how many houses have painted trusses in the attic?). Ancient history it was not. Enough of the structure survived the earlier fire so that the owners were forced to rebuild when insurance wouldn't pay for all.

The greatest later problem for these owners was that the house was breaking apart — an earlier intense summer storm had washed away packed dirt beneath the structure. Rather than replacing the firmer dirt, they used instead nearby sandy soil that was free-for-the-taking, even though I, as prospective buyer, was told, repeatedly, how they had carefully "piered" the house from beneath. The truth was that the weight of the house floated on a sandy base, which soon caused the structure to crack; it then began to seriously break apart. Even while I lived there, cracks began to widen and deepen in the floors and the front door became so skewed in its frame that the dead bolt rose a half-inch above its slot for alignment.

After I moved, they botched a job of patching the long, deep crack in the tile bathroom floor with conspicuously mismatched, tiny tiles — a sloppy attempt at deception intended for photos for the realtor's ads. The house lingered again on the market; then it was revealed that of the two country lots they had originally proposed to buy, these partners had paid for only one and had built the house on the wrong lot — the one they hadn't paid for — and thus the landowner was suing.

So it was burned again, this time more successfully, the owners no doubt illegally collecting insurance yet a second time. Dumber crooks could hardly be found, but as before, they were able to continue smugly on their way. The case was closed and there was little interest by the county in reopening an investigation.

I think of sleeping in my bed next to the wide windows with no curtains, my pups beside my bed and my cat Clovis sleeping on top with me; the dense woods a few feet beyond, no other house within a half-mile, and wonder if there, beyond my window, they stood in the dark, the grotesque, grinning landlord with a gasoline can next to him, a lighter at ready, his hand at work in his pants, all for dumb greed and his love of fire.

First Snow
Marble, Colorado

Dawn reveals
Raspberry Ridge
high above me,
its ridge line
now obscured in
slowly swirling clouds
of softly falling snow
and frozen mist.

Clinging to
its steep slope,
snow-encrusted pines,
their deep green
nearly black,
form a patchwork
with naked aspens,
leaden-hued
in this morning's
bleak light.

From far above,
snow casts in relief
the steep hillside's
folds and jagged fissures,
down which avalanches
have flowed, fearsome
in their power —

an onslaught of
snow and coursing
boulders carving
these deep creases
for many centuries past.

It's been a long
and restless night, with
no news of one
who is ill —
in a house miles
distant where
upper story lights
burned late.

From the
snowy boughs
of the yard's
tallest spruce, a
Steller's Jay
launches down
toward the ground,
wings exuberantly
extended,
primary flights
spread and ends
upturned —
yet, even its
iridescent, cobalt blue
seems muted

in this dawn's
dull light. . . .

But just now, in
emergent sunlight,
the Steller's again
chatters, swoops
back up
the tall spruce —
a bright, arcing,
metallic blue
cast against a yard
white with
yesterday's snow.

Her Hair

In the days
following her visit
  I looked for
  her footprint
    in dirt
to show where
we had walked;
  then, as winds
  sigh, snows settle,
    any traces
from that day were
    irretrievably lost.

  But today,
  with sunlight
streaming into the room
  where we sat,
I discovered there
  her hair —
a long, dark strand
  caught in a book,
  flowing forth
  in air, dancing
on a fan's breeze.

  With care,
  I hide away
this dark, wavy

  strand while
   longing for
  her presence —
her flesh, her bone,
her blood, her scent —
   from which I,
   and this hair,
    have lost
   connection.

My Great Cat Clovis, Afternoon Snow

In the bay window
he sits,
watching,
growing
ever wiser.

April Dawn
(Marble)

April first,
　light rain
　　at dawn,
White House Mountain
　nearly lost
　　in mist.
I woke early,
but this morning
　am allowed
　　sleeping in,
enjoy the warmth
　　of my bed.
　I ruminate on
　my present state,
　　searching for
　　　solutions.
As morning sun emerges,
　budding trees glistening
　　with raindrops
　　　offer hope
　　　　with this new
　　　　　Spring season.

Night light

As I ascend
my stairway
in darkness,
through the window
above me,
I see only
the glow
of moonlight
held within
delicate icicle
shafts.

The life of dreams

In a dream, one
 from long ago
 returns; we hug,
with deep affection,
 talk excitedly, while
 fully aware that
 this rare encounter
  quickly nears its end.
We weave away,
 together then apart,
through darkened corridors,
  hazy rooms, as
 the dream begins
  unraveling.

Upon waking,
 I'm grateful that
 life's long strands
  continue to connect
  in the realm of dreams;
yet wonder, is there really
  that silken dream world
  of fluid possibility?
   Or instead, only
   our starker reality?

Cold Spring

Cold, wet day;
  hot green tea,
    cup warm
  in my hands —
  all now bearable.

Marble
(Spring 2014)

Late morning,
a moose trots past
my house in this remote
 high mountain town.
My dogs' uncivil barking
 sends the moose cow
 on a frantic trot
 down our muddy street.

 Dusk, again walking,
 I pass a house long
 empty, paint peeling,
 sagging; through
 mottled windows
 above I see stacks
 of yellowed books
 in disarray, flanked
 by large, faded
 Greek letters, giving
 hints of learning
 that once resided there,
 a faint beacon
 of former erudition
 now long past.

 I know not now
 where I will be in

   two months' time, nor
     if I will ever
     live here again.

   The air grows sharply colder,
     yet retains ever longer
      the day's fleeting warmth,
       the promise of Spring.

At dusk, delicious scents
of sweet wood smoke linger
  in the slight breeze.
    In crepuscular sky
    I watch a plane track west,
      its blinking lights
       blending into
        emergent stars.

Year's End

Last morning
   of the old year —
      dull background
         of cloud,
            Raspberry Ridge
               above me
                  flattened against sky.

I worry for the new year,
   what we've done
       to our earth.

My mind wanders, west,
   to Oregon's coast —
      fog-wrapped, somber,
         grass glistening
            at ocean's edge,
               blue hydrangea globes
                  shimmering in mist.

Spring Snowstorm
(Sunday morning)

Varying from
    drops to
heavy wet flakes,
   moisture weeps
    from gauzy
     low cloud.

Marble Morning

Lying in bed late
on a day of rest,
listening to breezes
scrape pine boughs
against the house,
watching shadows
play against
my white lace curtains.
Across the way,
the last snows on
White House Mountain
melt, seep downward to
feed the churning
Crystal River.
Around me, mountainsides
are transformed green
with budding aspens.
Dewy red and white peonies
show tight flower bulbs
in the garden where
musky-scented lilacs
hang heavy with bloom.

Patio in Albi

A restaurant patio —
   Albi, light stone,
a warm February afternoon,
    sun daily
     gathering strength.

Looming above
   a bit distant,
the medieval
  box-like brick
   Cathédral Sainte-Cécile.

Having earlier absorbed
   hell's horrors
abound in its murals,
   we await lunch,
  appetites dampened.

   Here, in this
   Cathar stronghold,
Albigensian name source,
   personal troubles
    diminish along
stoney street canyons
that witnessed centuries
   of blood and strife.

In somber spirit one
   departs this city to
 seek solace amongst
    sun-cast green hills,
 broken rock houses lost
   in shadowy oak forest.

At Crestone Park
(for J&J)

Sunday morning,
we walk an icy trail
through woods
to the park, for
Jhana to play.

Behind us, in
the brilliant blue sky,
the cold gray
Sangre de Cristos peaks,
the Crestones,
are mottled with snow,
jagged, shimmering.

In another hour,
I must leave,
not knowing when,
if ever, we will
spend time
together again.

We travel swiftly
through life;
I am grateful for a
few fleeting moments
with friends to
hold as memory.

werewolves in deep night

"He who wears a bad coat needs only put it off."
  — Françoise La Hille, 18th Century southern French peasant woman, as complaint (1785–1787) against her neighbor who, she claimed, dressed in skins at night, posing as a werewolf, killing and threatening her cattle. (from *Jasmin's Witch* by Emmanuel Le Roy Ladurie)

In the dream world,
  sweet fennel to fend off
    witches' sorghum,
      but how to fight
        black sorcerer's
          fabricated charge, bribed
            by jealous lover's spite?

Hailed crops,
  litters lost,
    children stillborn,
    arms turned cold
      by a stranger's touch —
        who to blame but
          mandragore, poisoners,
            werewolves, witches?

    If only it were so easy —
      to cast off a bad coat,
        with it all aspersions,

aggressions, rude failings
wished to be
made right;

cattle could then thrive again,
all live lacking fear of
transgressions, agèd spite;
a clean wind would begin
sweeping our plain.

Prairie Sunset

Past peak,
a pinkish
gold glow
lingers across
western expanse
of sky —
then slowly
are spread
darker reds,
soft pinks,
clear yellows;
like fluids
in a wound,
congealing.

Poem on a morning with jam
(for Caroline)

I am reading poems
in a Yeats book
  while chewing a
  crusty French loaf
plastered with Spring grass
  Normandy butter and
  strawberry jam . . .

and as I feel
pages grown sticky,
   I pause,
not knowing if
I am on a green lawn
  sloping to lapping water
  and a hare's bone,
or am lunching on
   a shady French porch . . .
  or am here, in my chair,
   momentarily and
   blissfully unaware.

Supporting cast:
"The Collar Bone of a Hare" by William Butler Yeats
Pain de Campagne, Babette's Patisserie, Longmont, Colorado
Isigny Ste Mère Normandy Grass-Fed Spring Butter &
Bonne Maman Strawberry Preserves, products of France

The Wedding

A woman throws herself into a stream,
this stream throws itself into a river;
a man throws himself into the river,
this river throws itself into the sea,
and the sea throws up a foamy pipe
    onto the strand —
the white lace of the spreading wave
that shines beneath the moon
is a bride's gown,
    gifted by the tide.

1. Two White Feathers Fell From Sky

Sunday, mid-morning,
last day of October,
first morning of
deep Autumn chill.
I put out food
for the wild birds
and squirrels, stand in
the yard. Above, a low
mass of dull-white,
gauzy cloud; everywhere,
it is incredibly still.

I linger, reflecting,
comforted by stillness,
opaque thick air.

My eye catches
something white, like
a large snowflake, falling
straight from cloud —
instead, it is a
small white feather.
Before I can move to it,
another falls mere feet
from the first.

I pick up one, then
the other, examine them —

likely back or breast feathers,
from the same bird,
soiled slightly green.

I become aware that
what is most amazing
is that two feathers fell,
that I was there
to witness them.

From where
did they come?
Now-migrating
Sandhill Cranes
fly so high, their
ghostly chattering
nearly inaudible,
floating thousands
of feet to earth;
it seems unlikely,
nearly impossible,
that crane's feathers could
fall slowly together
so far down.

I heard no calls overhead,
no honking geese
in transit, nor quacks
from Mallard ducks
flying to the pond behind.

Likely a raptor attack,
silent, slashing —
are these feathers proof
of narrow escape?

I will never solve this
riddle from above,
however long I ponder —
it closes on itself,
much the same
as this still,
impenetrable day.

2. Two White Feathers Fell From Sky

From thick white cloud,
a white feather fell;
then, amazingly, another —
nothing more can be
known about them.
I have been gifted
imponderable mystery.

What's In a Name?
Reflections On Family, Lineage, and Matters of "Scribal Inattention" *

"In the time of the French Revolution, Pariseau, a ballet-master, was beheaded by mistake for Parisot, a captain of the King's Guard."
— Thomas Hardy, A Pair of Blue Eyes

*"What's in a name? that which we call a rose
By any other name would smell as sweet."*
— William Shakespeare, Romeo and Juliet

Juliet's wistfulness in reflecting upon her lover Romeo's name, the family name of her own family's enemy, is nearly universally known in the English-speaking world; the quote above from novelist Thomas Hardy is lesser-known but applies directly to my own family's name, which is *Perrizo* but is more historically accurate as *Pariseau* or *Parisot*. Although they are not entirely accurate either, as the original surname, we've learned, was *Delpech*, which in Occitan, the language of the ancient south of France, meant "from the hills." Or so it seems. The story is still being formed, woven from anecdotes, bits from history, nearly illegible entries in ancient documents, stories told that remain unconfirmed, even from carvings on long-buried stones later washed above ground.

---

* *Ermengard of Narbonne and the World of the Troubadours* by Frederic L. Cheyette, Cornell University Press, 2001, p. 227.

Our names are important for us in so many ways, but their importance as our identity is undeniable, even if their history is tenuous, inaccurate, nearly impenetrable or unknowable through long stretches of time. As a country of immigrants, we are long familiar with stories of family names arbitrarily and nonsensically changed at ports of entry like Ellis Island, with new legal names such as Johnson and Smith having no connection with sometimes centuries-old names brought from non-English speaking countries in Europe, Africa, Asia, and elsewhere. New residents, often with little or no money to start a new life in a new country, frequently made little effort to correct these errors and restore family names from their places of origin; in many instances they were long forgotten and recovered only when a member of a later generation became interested in "discovering" their family's history and came across documents that revealed a parent or grandparent's earlier life and former name in a distant country.

Because this is not intended to be a comprehensive study of these issues, I focus on my own family name, which may share some parallels to other families, or at least perhaps some of the frustrations with those whose name has been permanently altered with little reason.

Perrizo is our family name and the source of this reflection. Why does it matter?

I grew up in a southwestern Minnesota village where my name wasn't questioned and was amazingly pronounced correctly. I knew my Grandpa Perrizo was of French descent, his family was from the small town of Delavan in south-central Minnesota, where many French-Canadian settlers found a home in the late nineteenth century. We had the vague idea when growing up that our family name had been spelled differently, more "French" in previous times, and we thought that the spelling was "Pariseau." It was something of a surprise, then, when I took high school French to better understand my "heritage" and my teacher bluntly told me my name "Perrizo" was not French.

However, in matters of one's name and lineage, I realize now that I had mostly lived a charmed early life, as when I moved away from the small-town insularity and into the larger world, where I was confronted with people whose backgrounds included a larger swath of ethnicity than my small home town allowed, my name was rarely pronounced correctly again. When seeing my name spelled out, people immediately connected my name with an Italian ancestry and pronounced it as what they thought was accurate. And when bombarded by marketeers or others with no respect for one's heritage, my somewhat secure knowledge of who I was and from where I came was delivered a formidable blow.

Though to be authentically an Italian name, my *Perrizo* spelling would need two "z"s, this was a detail unknown to the horde of those wanting to sell something to "Pah-reee-zo," "Pah-right-zo," "Pah-ritzo," "Pizzarrio," "Pah-rize-oh," and countless other variations. While a manager and company officer at a scholarly book publisher, I began to receive, in the early days of computer-automated marketing, mail from one company that addressed me as: "Scott Perizzo," "Scott

Perinie," then "Scott Perinie-Perinie," and finally, in an obviously computer-generated promotion, "Scott Perinie-Perinie, Director of Art."

Hard to take were the mispronunciations from friends, coworkers, or especially a sneering top boss, after taking pains to make clear that the pronunciation of my name was like the French spelling *Pariseau*. Out of frustration, I sometimes told people at the other end of the phone line, who carelessly and repeatedly mispronounced the name after my careful attempts at giving them the correct pronunciation, that "if you're not interested in listening to me, then I don't have time to listen to you."

Over time, this becomes an assault on personal dignity, to a sense of self — and the sense of family, of heritage, of a family's place in the world.

In my own situation, I continually asked why did we have this family name "Perrizo" that we thought was a French name when the outer world nearly universally thought (insisted!) that we were of Italian origin? As it became obvious that the spelling "Perrizo" was the problem, I resolved to get answers. Obviously, the spelling *did not* seem French, even to me, so therefore the root fault of the mispronunciations must be the name's spelling.

It wasn't until my mid-forties that I first made contact with my distant cousin, Mitchel Perrizo Jr., who lived at Ashwood Farm outside Delavan, the south-central Minnesota village of French-Canadian and Irish immigrants where my grandfather was born and spent his early years. Ashwood Farm was the original family farm settled by Mitch's great-grandparents and grandparents in the 1860s — my great-great-grandfather Bruno owned a farm a half-mile or so down the road. Mitch had been a career Naval officer, retired from work at the Pentagon to live out his life at the family farm where he spent his youth. A very learned man and intellectual, in his eighties, he added a library wing to the old farmhouse, as the weight of his extensive collection of books in an upstairs room began to threaten the integrity of the overall structure.

Mitch was a wonderful resource, a man with a great sense of humor layered with his intelligence and life experience, and he was a meticulous keeper of records that included family history. We were close friends for over two decades before his death at 94 in 2011 and his encouragement and example changed the course of my life. Mitch connected me with Dr. Gordon Berry, a physicist who is now retired from teaching at Notre Dame University. Gordon was from Yorkshire and was a classmate at Oxford of Stephen Hawking and remained close friends with him his whole life. Gordon is married to Dr. Mary Hynes-Berry, my cousin whose mother was a Perrizo from Delavan. Aside from researching his own family, Gordon had assembled, and continues to do so, very comprehensive genealogical records tracing various branches of the Perrizo family back multiple generations to a common ancestor from France named Jean Delpech. All of this was beyond fascinating to me, as earlier I couldn't have conceived anything so remotely possible.

This common ancestor, Jean Delpech, was born in 1648 in the bishopric of Rodez in the south of France, an area known as the Rouergue; he became a soldier in the Carignan-Salières Regiment sent by Louis XIV in 1665 to New France, as the Iroquois tribes were disrupting the French fur trade in the newly settled parts of what is now Québec. The Regiment, famous in Canadian history, was based in the Montréal area and perhaps just their presence in the sparsely populated area was a greater deterrent to further raiding than any actual military engagement. After their mission was considered successful, they disbanded in 1668, with some Regimental members returning to France, while others were enticed to stay through offers of land, as New France was in dire need of permanent settlers. My ancestor, who had been only 16 when possibly impressed into service in 1665, perhaps lacked any reason to return to France, to his area in the south that had been hard hit by famines. Instead, he stayed in the Montréal area, married and raised a family; then in 1692, he was one of a group of settlers killed by an Iroquois raiding party at Pointe-aux-Trembles, the very east end of Montréal island. Contemporary reports had some of them being burned alive; my ancestor was likely one of them.

Jack Verney, author of *The Good Regiment*, told me in a 1998 phone conversation that most of the members of the Carignan-Salières Regiment were either northern French or Italian mercenaries and that it was rare for someone from the south, like our ancestor, to have been part of the Regiment. There was, however, another Regimental member from the south named Bernard Delpesches dit Belair, who was from Tonnac, a village in the Tarn, roughly thirty miles south of the village of Parisot, Tarn-et-Garonne, where we came to believe that our ancestor was born. As the father of both our Jean and this Bernard was also named Jean Delpech (they had different mothers), it has long been my hunch that they could have been half-brothers and joined the Regiment together (or were impressed into service together), but any records supporting that conclusion have not yet been discovered.

In the Regiment, many soldiers were given "dit" names, which were like nicknames added to their surnames, often reflecting their home villages. My ancestor was recorded in the Rolls of the Regiment as Jean Delpech dit Parisot, which is a very good clue as to his place of origin. And this "Parisot," a soldier's nickname, is the source of our own "surname" now spelled Perrizo.

Why Parisot? Though his marriage certificate from 1672 to Renée Lorion in Montréal gave the bishopric of Rodez (*évêché de Rodez*) in France as his origin, the village of Parisot, Tarn-et-Garonne, was indeed part of the larger area covered in the bishopric of Rodez at that time. In the many Canadian histories dealing with the members of the Regiment and early settlement in Québec, his birthplace was most often given as Rodez, indicating the city in the region, yet there became growing reason to believe that was not accurate.

Other points of confusion seemed to be passed along in the Canadian histories, notably that the Jean Delpech dit Parisot from the Rolls of the Carignan-Salières Regiment was later recorded variously as Jean Delpé dit Pariseau, Jean Delpue (or Delpuer) dit Pariseau, or Jean Dalpé dit Pariseau, as well as other even more incomprehensible variations. The origins of these later alterations, I feel, stem from the very hard to read handwriting on the marriage certificate of 1672, as Jean's name on that document does indeed look like "Delpue," but that seems, at least to me, a product of the scribe officiating, a very long flourish of the hand at the end of the name now obscured further by time in the hard to read microfiche copy of the document I first viewed in the archives in Montréal in 1999. No further clarification is really possible when viewing digital copies of the document now available on-line.

After much research, we began to focus on this Parisot village in the south of France as the more possible birthplace of our ancestor instead of Rodez, as no relevant records were found at Rodez to confirm it as the place of his birth. In September 1998, our first trip was made to France and the village of Parisot in the south to seek records, documents, or any other form of proof.

At the Departmental Archives of Aveyron in Rodez in 1998, I was able to have photocopied in its entirety the book *Parisot* by Joseph Lombard (1902). This history of the village gives evidence of various Delpech family members present at the village of Parisot, Tarn-et-Garonne, in years relevant to our Jean Delpech possibly being born there in 1648. There were also some Delpech family members at the hamlet below the village now called Lacau, but in earlier times called Localme, or even earlier, Clopservel. And interesting for our search, in the hamlet Causseviel a short distance farther, there was evidence of the Delnau or Delnat family, as the mother of our ancestor Jean Delpech was given as Marguerite Delnau. This circumstantial but unprovable evidence gave greater credence to Parisot village as the birthplace of Jean Delpech.

And on that 1998 trip, on a chilly Sunday morning in the street just below the village church St Andéol (completed in the late 1400s), cousin Bill Hoffman and I obtained a helpful clue during a short conversation with a possible family connection. A former villager named Jean-Louis Delpech had returned that day to visit his sister in the village — Jean-Louis lived a two-hour drive south, at Blagnac, location of the international airport for Toulouse. Jean-Louis mentioned a Canadian who had visited the village a few years earlier, which would turn out to be very helpful information. And in meeting Jean-Louis Delpech that morning, a white-haired but active man in perhaps his late 60s, I immediately and indescribably sensed something familiar, an impalpable connection to a possible family member despite the separation of many generations through many centuries.

Not long after returning from that 1998 trip, I was able to make contact with Dr. Jean Pariseau, a Canadian military historian living in Ottawa — he was indeed the man who had visited Parisot village earlier and had met Jean-Louis Delpech. In disagreement with the Canadian histories who gave numerous variations to the surname of our ancestor and gave his birthplace as Rodez, Dr. Jean Pariseau agreed with us that our ancestor was originally named Jean Delpech and was born in 1648 at the village of Parisot, Tarn-et-Garonne. This was significant contemporary affirmation by a scholar and historian, one studying his own family history independently but who arrived at the same conclusions that we did, despite contrary documentation in the popular Canadian histories. Dr. Jean Pariseau was descended from Pierre, the last son from the marriage of our soldier ancestor Jean Delpech dit Parisot to Renée Lorion, while my family was descended from François, their second son. In an eerie coincidence, a photo of Dr. Jean in his early years while in his Canadian Air Force uniform looks amazingly like photos of my own father from the same period in his life. (Even more amazing, a photo of a young man leading a horse in Parisot village in France in the early 1940s, in a book I purchased on that 1998 trip, looked so much like my own Dad at a similar age that it could have been him in the photo.)

While all this was very interesting to me and to a few family members, what did it mean in the grander scheme of things? And what did it do to solve the riddle of why our family name was Perrizo, which didn't look at all French in origin?

All of the many new details that we found initially confused matters more, due to the numerous variations to our ancestor's name that were given him after his arrival in New France. Jean Delpech was given the soldier's nickname "dit Parisot" when he became a soldier in the

Carignan-Salières Regiment in 1665, then possibly saw his "official" name change even in his own lifetime to Jean Delpech dit *Pariseau*, which author Jack Verney told me was likely the result of the mostly Norman French population of Montréal in the seventeenth century who would have used the *-eau* ending (Parisot is thought to have been originally *Castellum de Parisotum*, from Roman times, which may have possibly been the name of the Roman commander of the fortified hill-top village that became Parisot). Delpech is still a common name in the southwest of France, its origin is thought to be from the Occitan language, and meant "from the hills." Occitan, the ancient language of the south of France, was still taught in the village school at Parisot at the time of our first visit in 1998.

In 2002, at the Regional Archives for Tarn-et-Garonne in Montauban, Dr. Gordon Berry and I were able to photograph many relevant pages from the heavy, large-format, dusty cadastre records for Parisot commune from 1578 and 1644, pages showing in an expansive, flowing script many Delpech family members owning property in the area; there were, however, no variations of the surname like "Delpuech," which is also a common and similar name in the southwest of France. Notably, we found none of the later changes to the Delpech name that became commonplace after our ancestor settled in the New World.

Changes that happened later in the Montréal area were when the original surname Delpech became truncated to Delpé, Dalpé, then into many other later variations, such as Dubé, Duby, Dolby, Dubec, Dolbec, etc., and the original nickname Parisot became Pariseau, Parizeau, Pariso, and two hundred years later for my own branch of the family, Perrizo. The descendants of Jean Delpech dit Parisot split into sub-families who took some variation of the original Delpech name and others who took some variation of the "dit" name, or his soldier's nickname for his village.

These variations can mostly be attributed, I think, to an often non-literate population having their official events recorded by various clerks, scribes, and keepers of legal records. As the records were handwritten, the "hand" of the scribe, sometimes difficult to read but also at times beautifully inscribed, often with great flourishes and embellishments, became the official record. The material used for the pages as well as storage methods for the records further subjected these official documents to deterioration over time and a resultant lack of clarity.

Official records for an individual sometimes had only a tenuous relation to that person's former name or history. A name's recorded version that survived the centuries became the official spelling of the name, with the history of how it became so lost along the way. When French-speaking families like ours immigrated to the U.S. in the 1840s to seek a better life, they were at the mercy of the English-speaking recorder of their names and other official details of their life.

Much information has been gathered to be considered, but disappointingly, the total picture remains murky. Tantalizing details have emerged — on the 1998 trip, we became acquainted with an American couple and their son who lived in an ancient moulin (flour mill) south of Parisot village. I am still friends with them today and have twice stayed in their lovely and ancient mill home while housesitting for them. In 2003, during an intense summer rainstorm, some large, heavy millstones were washed up in the field near the mill. They were obviously the older, worn grinding stones put into the field after they were no longer of service; on one of them was carved "Garic Delpech 1819." One never knows where a search like this will take one, but it is unusual to have relevant details so serendipitously wash up out of the ground in a summer rain storm after being buried over a hundred years.

As for any historical documents in the village of Parisot itself to lend credence to our search? Aside from those village cadastre records at the archives in Montauban, no birth, death, or marriage records seem available and we were once told that in the 1940s, the village records were destroyed, having been kept in the small village church St Andéol. The story was that the church caretaker took in someone who needed shelter and let him stay in the church. As it was cold, this person, who was said to be "not right in the head," had taken the records, page by page, and burned them to keep warm. I am not at all convinced that this story is credible, but actual and pertinent village records have eluded us, for whatever reason.

All of this could have ended as the delightful but inconclusive result of searching for one's family and the source of one's name, but inevitably, more information turns up. After years of researching and not ever finding clues as to why, through all the variations of spelling through hundreds of years, our branch of the family became Perrizo, what seems a very plausible explanation just came to light in late 2021. Cousin Bill Hoffman was sent the citizenship documents for two family members, father and son, from 1849 in Fond du Lac, Wisconsin. The family had settled in Fond du Lac for a few years after leaving the Montréal area and entering the U.S. at Rouses Point, New York, about 1846. We know that the family members who arrived at Fond du Lac were French-speaking with perhaps minimal or no English-language skills and that at the time of their arrival in Fond du Lac, their family name had been "Dalpé dit Pariseau." Apparently encountering English-only recorders of documents when seeking citizenship in 1849, the two family members in these documents were both named Michel Dalpé dit Pariseau and were recorded as Mitchell Perrizo Sr. and Mitchell Perrizo Jr. A year later, the 1850 U.S. Census in Fond du Lac County, Wisconsin, has the father, the former Michel Dalpé dit Pariseau, registered as Michael Parisa, even though he was officially Mitchell Perrizo Sr. a year earlier on his U.S. citizenship documentation. And all his sons listed in that 1850 Census, including my great-great-grandfather Bruno, were recorded as "Parisa," except one, Hubert, who kept the Dalpé version as surname and that family still uses Dalpé to this day. From that time on, all others in my branch of the family have used the spelling they were arbitrarily assigned in 1849 — Perrizo.

My cousin Mitch Perrizo Jr. told me the story that a group of younger family members attending Delavan High School at the end of the nineteenth century wanted to change *en masse* the spelling of Perrizo back to Pariseau. Mitch said that their parents told them that if they had to put up with Perrizo, these children would too, and the name remained unchanged going forward.

At the time recently that I was sent those digital copies of the 1849 and 1850 documents that seemed, finally, to show the origin of the Perrizo spelling of our name, I was also very much engrossed in reading a well-researched and copiously documented history by Frederic L. Cheyette, *Ermengard of Narbonne and the World of the Troubadours*. In trying to describe how an Occitan fief in twelfth-century France was different in the social realm from the normal understanding of how a fief functioned in the social hierarchy, Cheyette admits that the usage in that case was rare and could be attributed to "merely the result of scribal inattention." I thought that this was a wonderful phrase and could be used more generally, such as in the case of my family name being changed to Perrizo by a clerk in 1849 in Fond du Lac County, Wisconsin, or in countless instances for so many others. The phrase "scribal inattention" could see many substitutions for the word "inattention": perhaps incompetence, arrogance — the list could go on.

"Scribal maliciousness" or "scribal mischievousness" might also be added. My sister Gail related a story from Minneota, Minnesota, where she lives, a small town that is one of

North America's most notable settlements of Icelandic immigrants. The story was told of an Icelandic family there named "Frost," a name reportedly given to them by a port-of-entry record-taker or scribe who proclaimed, perhaps out of frustration after a long day of trying to understand the Icelanders, that the next person in line would be entered in the records as "Jack Frost" — Iceland being a cold land and such. And Frost they have been ever since.

In the twenty-first century, family and heritage has become big business, with many companies offering DNA testing or ancestry tracing. Whether we are being provided accurate information perhaps remains to be seen, but many are eager to discover their past and the lives of predecessors who have shared their name.

In other examples of family as business, many years ago my uncle showed me a brochure he had received that pitched a coat of arms for the Perrizo family — unless that coat of arms was prepared by that Fond du Lac county clerk who changed our name's spelling to Perrizo, then that offer had no basis in fact. And recently, my sister Gail sent me a targeted marketing brochure for black hoodies, pint beer glasses, and hats emblazoned with a bright red graphic of Italy's outline and the slogan: "PERRIZO, American made from the finest Italian parts."

In 1991, frustrated by the endless mispronunciations, I told my cousin Mitch Perrizo, Jr., of my very strong desire to change the spelling of Perrizo to the more French-looking and easier to pronounce Pariseau. Mitch replied in his thoughtful way, "Make certain you know what you would change it to." Little did I know then that the matter wasn't so cut and dried. I did begin using the Pariseau spelling for email addresses, as the name for my pigeon loft in the pigeon hobby, and as my author's name for my writing, including this book — it made me feel that I was taking back something that had been taken from me. Now I know that Pariseau, as my historical family name, is perhaps only slightly more accurate than Perrizo. And to officially change one's name in this century is a far more complicated task than it was for the clerk who made my family Perrizo. At this late stage of my life, despite all my earlier intentions, I am not sure if I still have the resolve to follow through. However, with every new mispronunciation of the name, knowing what I now know about this history, my motivation is renewed.

My cousin Caroline Parizeau's wise son Jack, in his early teens, tells her that we are a way for the universe to experience itself. In trying to come to terms with my own nearly life-long struggle with my name and its possible meaning, I must admit that it has not been without some rather great benefits and unexpected moments of enjoyment. Through my search, I have met relatives and made friends that I wouldn't otherwise have known; I've traveled to places I might not have visited; I have visited four times already (and hope for more) my ancestral village Parisot, a lovely medieval village in the beautiful, historic, and rather off-the-beaten-track countryside of southwest France; I became familiar with the Montréal area in a meaningful way; I have gained a much deeper understanding of history and of who I am, what names and families mean, and how we function in the grand scheme of life. And so, if the universe has allowed me this as part of experiencing itself, I will always remain most deeply grateful.

Autumn Dawn

Early bright sunlight,
streaking low between
tree trunks,
transforms luminous
grass still heavy
with frost.

Within this calm,
still moment,
from every tree
around me
leaves flutter
softly to ground.

Wings clapping
loudly, exuberantly,
pigeons lift skyward
for brisk morning flight.

Our Evolution

My eyes registered the flat, rectangular patch just before my car's tire rolled over it.

A soft "Tha-Thunk."

The small strip had a bit of hairy white on top, worn away by countless cars passing over it. A rabbit most likely, a hapless victim while crossing the road. I think of the many centuries of genetic evolution that brought forth the soft, living being that is now a hardened bit of pelt on the road — animal life carried across countless generations to be placed by time in front of a car to be flattened into an unrecognizable carcass on the asphalt. In a spot on the road that was once a grassy trail where earlier its ancestors passed freely.

Motorized vehicles are too newly introduced for wildlife to yet evolve to avoid them; perhaps, before it's too late, they will.

I'm reminded of how African elephants are very recently evolving to become tuskless in a remarkable genetic adaptation, in real time, to evade poachers seeking their ivory.

I'm also reminded of hearing how, in reaction to highway overpasses being constructed for wildlife crossings at longstanding migratory trails now interrupted by high-speed traffic, someone had objected to their placement as an inconvenience and wondered if they might be moved elsewhere?

As the human population continues to either ignore or ineffectively grapple with the human-caused problems of our warming planet, we move toward eventually ending habitability on our only home. Earth might eventually become an oven planet like Venus, our neighbor that once held oceans and may have supported life before overheating, its water then evaporating. Laughable are the recent highly publicized escapades of billionaires fueled on Star Wars fantasies, gaining entry into space with the longer-term goal of finding a new home when we've destroyed this one.

In so many ways, humans on this planet behave like loud, rowdy drunks at a frat party, intoxicated beyond all sense of place and reason, partying through the night while trashing the house and trying to tear it down — it makes only good sense that the host, our Mother Earth, has no choice but throw our sorry asses out.

Perhaps it is already too late to enact measures to save this planet for the continuation of life on it, even if we could agree on them. But it is imperative that we recognize the seriousness of our situation and change our ways now, even if it means that we die trying.

We really have no other options left. We are running out of luck, we are running out of time, we are moving beyond hope; our planet does not need us and will be better off without a human presence. But we obviously need our planet and recognizing that simple and profound truth is our only path to survival. Whether we succeed will be shown by our continued, integrative presence on our host planet or in archeological records, fossilized for some later civilization to discover and interpret what might have been our profound folly, the possible reasons lost to the ages.

A New Year

Afternoon, an odd light,
horizontal bands
of gauzy cloud
in relief against
deep blue sky.
Calm, drinking raspberry-
flavored green tea,
remembering on this third day
of the new year that
some years past,
I lost my great dog, Lea,
so close to me from her birth
into my waiting hands
until that day of her death.

I open the box with her ashes,
touch the cream- and fawn-colored
hair I've kept there,
hair that I clipped
when she was gone.

I have other dogs now,
my cats and pigeons too —
all, past and present,
deeply a part of my life.
At the end, I want to
take them all with me

in a flat-bottomed boat,
skim skyward
into the stars.

A Poet's Epitaph

So many words withheld
to say so very few . . .

About the Author

Born in Minneapolis, Scott Pariseau was raised on the southwestern Minnesota prairie. After moving to Oregon for a year, he has since lived most of his life in various places on Colorado's Front Range and Western Slope, with a brief one-year interlude in Oklahoma. His first jobs while young included working for farmers baling hay, picking rocks from fields, hand-pulling cockleburs and thistles from corn and soy bean fields, cleaning hog barns — he remembers that his first job was picking up corn cobs blown down in fields during an Autumn storm, for which he was paid 20 cents an hour, and that he was so small he could barely carry the heavy bucket of corn. He also mowed lawns, including his church lawn and cemetery, worked in a grocery store, pumped gas and changed tires.

Later, he spent a career in the publishing industry: worked for newspapers; was an assistant vice president for a scholarly book publisher; a typographer, book designer, editor and proofreader; a production manager for book publishers; a computer systems manager; a customer service and sales representative for printing companies. He even had a brief stint as a museum curator and a cheese monger. He lives again in the Boulder area with his treasured companions — wonder cat Pippin, Shelties Bronwen and Anachie, Afghan Hound Spyder-Mae, and various English Trumpeter and homing pigeons.